Daily
Bread

Compiled and Edited by

Judith Bosley

Cover and Illustrations by

Steve Miles

L.E.B. Inc.
Boise, Idaho

Many thanks to Klara Chwastek for suggesting the title for this book and for contributing her favorite recipes.

L.E.B. Inc.
5375 Kendall Street
Boise, Idaho 83706

YES YOU CAN!

Yes, you can bake your own bread, sweet rolls, and muffins. You can make your own pancakes and waffles (known as "awfuls" in our family, baked in Grandma's "awful" iron.) You can make English muffins and bagels. Yes, they take a little time, but they are not hard at all. You can make hot cross buns for Easter, and fancy Christmas breads for gifts. You can try the breads of other countries, because everywhere on earth, some form of bread is the staff of life.

One very important element of bread baking, attested to by most bread makers is its therapeutic value. God alone knows how much anxiety and frustration, anger and grief has been kneaded into bread dough. Bread dough has probably been a marriage saver, a child abuse preventative and a life preserver for as long as men and women have pounded flour and water together and baked the loaf for the family meal. The basic need to bake bread even when there isn't time is demonstrated by the popularity of bread machines now used by many. I have included recipes for those bakers too. And for others with limited time and energy, there are quick breads, and even quicker breads.

Yes, there are a few things to learn. These are easy, sensible and if you do something differently than directed, it doesn't matter. Your product may just be a little lighter, heavier or different tasting, but I can almost guarantee that your family will gobble it up just the same. Bread making is not an exact science and there is no way to learn except by doing it. No one can tell you the exact amount of flour to use or how long the dough will take to rise in your kitchen. Who knows if you like your crust dark and crisp, or light gold and buttery. Have it your own way.

Tips for Quick Breads; breads without yeast

Flour: Flour measurements need to be accurate with quick breads; too much flour can make a heavy product. It usually is not necessary to sift flour if you understand that flour compacts. Spoon flour lightly into a measuring cup, filling it over full, and level off with a knife.

Method: Sugar and shortening are usually creamed together; eggs and fruits, vegetables and other flavoring agents are added. Flour is then stirred in but the batter is not beaten. Over beating will make muffins, pancakes and quick breads tough. Stir only until mixed, then put into baking pans.

Baking: Quick breads are sometimes heavy with fruit or other ingredients, so they require a fairly long baking time. Test for doneness with a tooth pick inserted in loaf; when toothpick comes out clean, bread is done.

Tips for Yeast Breads

Flour: Flour measurements are approximate. Generally, you stir flour into liquid ingredients containing dissolved yeast until liquid is absorbed and a dough is formed. Then additional flour is spread on any flat, clean surface, such as a table, counter top or bread board. The dough is turned out of the mixing bowl and additional mixing, called kneading, is done with the hands.

Kneading: Don't put your fingers *into* the dough, rather, push and fold the dough on the floured board, adding more flour when necessary so that dough does not stick to hands or board. Keep kneading and folding until dough becomes smooth and "elastic." Elastic means that it gets springy.

Yeast: There is no mystery about using yeast. It is a live plant and must be kept alive to make bread raise. Do not kill the action of yeast by putting it in very hot water, or in a hot oven until it has done its work. Most bakers use dry yeast because of the convenience. Others prefer compressed yeast cakes. In both cases, yeast is usually dissolved in warm, not hot water. Then the yeast and water are added to other liquids in the recipe. There is quick-rise yeast on the market that is not dissolved in water, but mixed with the flour and then very warm liquids are added to the dry ingredients. Just follow the directions on the package.

Raising the dough: The yeast does this, not the baker. You just make the conditions right. After dough is mixed, it should be covered with a clean towel. Perfect conditions are a warm, (not hot), draft free place in your kitchen. If the room is cold, you can turn your oven on for a minute, turn it off and place dough in oven to raise.   Dough will rise in the refrigerator, but much more slowly.

Most doughs raise twice, once after the first mixing; then again after the dough is made into a loaf. Sometimes it raises only once, as in batter breads that are quite coarse in texture. Dough can be punched down and allowed to raise a third time; a method used for fine grained breads like French bread. When loaves are ready for the oven, handle carefully or they can collapse. If dough does collapse, there is nothing to do except remove it from the pans, fold into loaves again and let it rise again.

Topping the loaf: For a dull, crusty loaf, brush top of bread with water near the end of baking. For a shiny, soft crust, brush hot loaf with melted butter or margarine. For a shiny, crusty loaf beat an egg with a little water and brush top of loaf before or during baking.

Baking: Yeast breads require a much shorter baking time than quick breads. A loaf of yeast bread should bake in 25-35 minutes. One way to test for doneness is to tap top or bottoms of loaf, and it should sound hollow. Another method is to tip loaf out of pan and check to see if bottom is browned and looks done, if not, replace in pan and bake a little longer.

BREADS

PANCAKES, BISCUITS, DUMPLINGS & CRACKERS

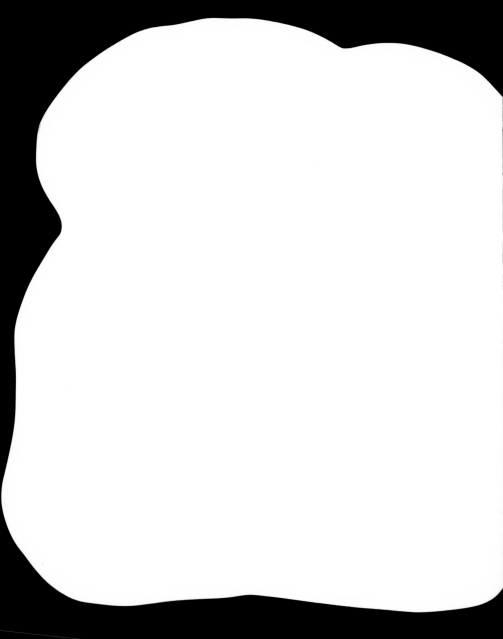

1 HOMEMADE PANCAKES & WAFFLES

Easy as using a mix, and "so" much better

2 C flour	2 eggs, beaten
5 t baking powder	2 C milk
2 t salt	5 T oil
3 T sugar	

Combine dry ingredients and stir in liquids; Stir just until blended.
Batter will be lumpy. Bake on a hot, greased griddle.
12 pancakes.

>*Pancake variations:* Prepare pancake batter as above or from a
mix. Stir in 1 cup blueberries or chopped apple, 1/2 C raisins or
chopped nuts.

>*Waffles:* Add only egg yolks to batter; beat egg whites until stiff
and fold into batter last. Bake on a hot, greased or sprayed waffle
iron. 12 waffles.

√See also *"Quicker Breads"* for more pancakes and waffles.

2 BUTTERMILK PANCAKES

2 C flour
2 T sugar
2 C buttermilk
1 t salt

2 T oil
2 eggs
1 t soda

Mix all ingredients and bake on a greased griddle.

3 CORN MEAL PANCAKES

1 C yellow corn meal
1 t salt
1 T sugar
1 C boiling water
1 egg

1/2 C milk
2 T butter, melted
1/2 C white flour
2 t baking powder

Place corn meal, salt, and sugar in bowl. Stir while slowly adding boiling water. Cover and let stand 10 minutes. Beat egg, milk and melted butter; add to cornmeal. Stir remaining dry ingredients into batter, stirring only until blended. Bake cakes on a greased, hot griddle.

4 OAT PANCAKES

1 C flour
1/2 C quick oats
2 t baking powder
1/2 t salt

1 egg
1 C milk
2 T butter
2 T sugar

Combine dry ingredients in a bowl. Beat egg and milk together and add to dry ingredients. Melt butter on griddle, then pour into batter and stir to combine. Pour 1/3 cup batter onto hot buttered griddle for each pancake, adding butter as needed. Bake until bubbles form and hold on surface; turn and brown other side. Serve with butter and maple syrup. 6 pancakes.

5 BREAD CRUMB PANCAKES

Light, both in texture and calories

1 C soft bread crumbs
1/3 C dry milk powder
2/3 C hot water
1 T oil

1 beaten egg
1/3 C flour
3/4 t baking powder
1/4 t salt

Combine bread crumbs, milk powder, water and oil; let stand 5 minutes. Stir in remaining ingredients and bake on a sprayed griddle. Serve with butter, syrup or low calorie jam.

6 CHERRY PANCAKES

Use fresh, canned, dried, frozen, sweet or sour cherries

2 C flour
5 t baking powder
2 t salt
3 T sugar

2 eggs
2 C milk
6 T oil
1/2-1 C cherries

Mix dry ingredients and stir in eggs, milk and oil just until blended. Pour batter onto a hot, greased griddle and drop 5-6 cherries on each pancake. Turn cakes to bake other side. Sprinkle with white sugar or serve with cherry sauce.

Cherry sauce:
1 C cherry juice
1 T cornstarch
1/2 t salt

1/3 C sugar
1 T butter
2-3 drops red food coloring

Combine ingredients in a saucepan and cook until thick and clear.

7 JEANENE'S BAKED APPLE PANCAKE

Put it all together; it spells delicious breakfast for four

2 apples, thinly sliced
4 T butter or margarine
1/2 C flour
1/2 t salt
1/4 t nutmeg

4 eggs
1/2 C milk
1 T sugar
1 t cinnamon

Heat oven to 450°. Melt butter in a 10-12 inch heavy skillet and sauté apple slices until just tender. Combine flour, salt, nutmeg, eggs and milk in mixer or blender and beat for 2 minutes. Immediately pour batter over sizzling butter and apples and bake for 12-15 minutes or until edges are puffed and brown. Combine sugar and cinnamon and sprinkle over pancake. Return to oven for 3-5 minutes more. Serves 4.

8 BEST EVER BISCUITS

These never fail, and never fail to please

2 2/3 C sifted flour
1 t salt
2 1/2 t baking powder

1/2 t soda
1/2 C butter or margarine
1 C buttermilk

Combine dry ingredients; cut in butter or margarine with a pastry cutter until mixture resembles coarse meal. Stir in buttermilk with a fork. Turn onto a floured board and cut biscuits. Bake on an ungreased baking sheet at 450° for 12-15 minutes until golden. 12-16 biscuits.

9 CHEESE BISCUITS

2 C flour
4 t baking powder
1 t salt

2 T shortening
7/8 C milk
3/4 C shredded sharp cheddar

Combine dry ingredients and cut in shortening and cheese; Stir in milk with a fork. Pat out on a floured board and cut biscuits. Bake at 400° for 15 minutes.

10 ENGLISH TEA SCONES

An easy to make delicacy

2 C flour
2 T sugar
3 t baking powder
1/2 t salt

1/3 C dried currants
6 T butter or margarine
1 beaten egg
1/2 C milk

Combine dry ingredients and stir in currants. Cut in butter until mixture is the consistency of coarse meal. Add combined egg and milk, stirring just until flour is dampened. Turn onto a floured board and knead slightly. Pat dough 3/4 inch thick into a rectangle; cut into 4 inch squares, then cut the squares diagonally into triangles. Place wedges on an ungreased baking sheet and brush with beaten egg. Bake at 400°- 425° 12-15 minutes. 12 scones.

√The less biscuit dough is handled, the more tender and flaky it will be.

11 NEW STYLE SHORTCAKE

2 C flour
3 T sugar
3 t baking powder
1 t salt

1/3 C oil
2/3 C milk

Mix oil and milk. Combine dry ingredients and add liquid all at once. Stir with a fork until mixture forms a ball. Turn onto a floured board; pat out 3/4 inch thick and cut into rounds with a floured glass or cookie cutter. Bake on an ungreased cookie sheet at 475° for 10-12 minutes.

12 OLD - FASHIONED SHORTCAKE

2 C flour
3 t baking powder
3/4 t salt

1/4 C brown sugar
1/2 C butter or margarine
1/2 C milk (or more)

Combine dry ingredients and cut in butter with a pastry blender. Make a well in center and add milk all at once. Stir with a fork just until dough cleans the side of the bowl; use slightly more milk if needed. Turn dough onto a lightly floured board and knead 10 times. Pat dough into a greased layer cake pan, or cut small biscuits. Bake at 450° for 20 minutes.

13 MULESKINNER FRIED BISCUITS

With muleskinner measurements. The hot grease they are cooked in is the shortening. Really good!

1 C flour
1 rounded teaspoon sugar
2 heaping teaspoons baking powder
pinch salt
water to make a stiff batter
hot grease; lard, bacon fat, beef grease are all used to vary flavor

Drop batter into hot grease, about 1/4 inch deep. Turn when brown. Makes about 6 biscuits, 1/2 inch thick. Serve hot.

√Try sprinkling biscuits with poppy or sesame seed before baking, or make raisin faces for school lunch boxes.

14 BUTTERSCOTCH BISCUITS

A quickie dessert

2 C flour
3 t baking powder
1/2 t salt
4 T butter

7/8 C milk
1/3 C butter
3/4 C brown sugar
1/2 C nutmeats

Combine flour, baking powder and salt; cut in 4 tablespoons butter with a pastry blender. Add milk and stir until blended. Blend butter and brown sugar. Roll dough into a rectangle, spread with sugar and butter mixture. Sprinkle with nuts. Roll as for a jelly roll, cut in 1 inch slices and place in greased muffin cups. Bake at 400° for 12-15 minutes. Invert on waxed paper. Serve warm.

15 DROP DUMPLINGS

Delicious puffs in your soup

1 C sifted flour
1 1/2 baking powder
3/4 t salt

1/2 t sugar
1/2 C milk
1 egg

Combine dry ingredients. Beat egg with milk and stir into dry ingredients until blended. Drop mixture into hot soup or stew. Cover and cook for 10-12 minutes.

16 NORWEGIAN DUMPLINGS

*Light as air dumplings, or make cream puffs!**

1/4 C butter
1 C boiling water
1 C flour

2 large eggs
1/4 t salt
1/4 t nutmeg

Combine butter and water in a sauce pan and bring to a boil; add flour and mix well. Cook about 2 minutes, stirring constantly; cool to lukewarm. Add eggs one at a time, stirring well. Drop by tablespoons into soup. Cook covered for 15-20 minutes.

***Cream Puffs:** After desired amount of batter is used for dumplings, drop remaining batter by large spoonsful on an ungreased baking sheet and bake at 400° for 45-50 minutes. Cool and fill with cream filling.*

√Another kind of dumpling is added to Hungarian soups. Make a thick paste of egg and flour; put mixture on a plate and cut off small pieces into the soup, dipping knife into the soup as you snip off the pieces. Continue cooking until "csipetke" rises to top.

17 LAVASH

Homemade crackers; crunchy and delicious

3 2/3 C flour (use part whole wheat)
2 T poppy seed
1 1/2 t salt
1 t sugar
1/2 t onion powder
1/2 t garlic powder
1/3 C sesame seed, toasted

1/3 C oil
1 egg, slightly beaten
1 C skimmed milk

Combine dry ingredients in a large bowl; add poppy seed.
Combine oil, egg and milk and stir into flour mixture, mixing well.
Cover dough and let rest for 30 minutes. Sprinkle 3-4 baking
sheets with sesame seed. Divide dough and roll each portion
very thin, as for pie crust, rolling again after it is on pans and
patting with floured hands to get it thinner. Score with a knife for
breaking into pieces after baking. Bake at 375° for 20-25 minutes
until slightly browned and crisp. Cool, break into pieces.

*Vary herbs and seasonings to suit taste

18 OATMEAL CRACKERS

Flavorful; grain flavors need no other seasonings

3 C oatmeal, either old fashioned or quick cooking
1 C wheat germ
2 C flour
1 1/2 T sugar
1 t salt
3/4 C oil
1 C water

Combine ingredients well. Divide dough in half and roll as thinly as possible onto 3 ungreased cookie sheets. Cut into squares and sprinkle lightly with coarse salt. Bake at 300° for 30 minutes or until crisp and lightly browned.

√To freshen stale crackers, spread crackers on a baking sheet and place in oven that has just been turned off. Cool and put in plastic bags.

19 GRAHAM CRACKERS

Yes, you and the kids can make your own

2 C whole wheat flour
1/2 C margarine
2 T sugar
2 T honey
1/2 t soda
1/2 t cream of tartar
1 egg white
1/4-1/3 C water (about)
white flour for rolling

Cut margarine into flour with a pastry blender until well blended.
Add sugar, honey, soda, cream of tartar, egg white and enough
water to make a dough that will hold together like pastry. With
floured hands and rolling pin, roll and pat as thinly as possible onto
ungreased baking sheets. Cut into squares and bake at 350° for
15-20 minutes or until crackers begin to brown. Cool on a rack.
Makes about 24, 3 inch crackers.

**MUFFINS,
QUICK BREADS
& COFFEE CAKES**

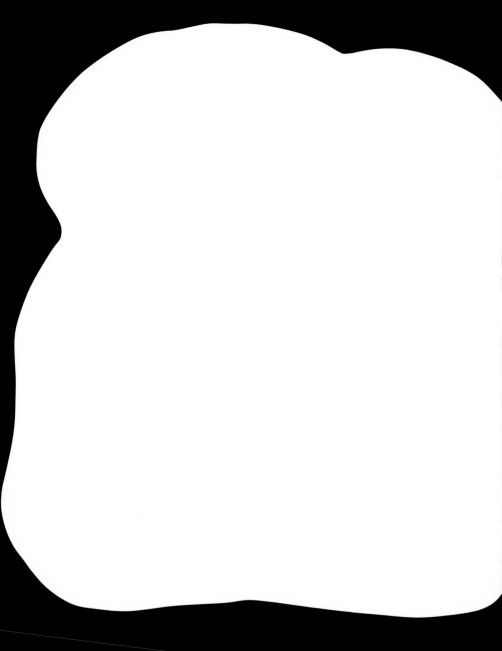

20 CORN FRITTERS

1 C flour
2 eggs
1/2 C milk
1/2 evaporated milk

2 C whole kernel corn
1/2 C chopped green onions
1/2 C grated cheddar cheese
2-4 T oil for frying

Combine flour, eggs, milk and evaporated milk; beat until smooth.
Stir in remaining ingredients. Heat oil in a heavy skillet; Drop
mixture by tablespoons in oil and spread slightly. Fry until golden
on both sides. About 30 fritters.

21 HUSH PUPPIES

1 1/2 C corn meal
3 T flour
1 t salt
1/2 t pepper

1 egg
1 small onion, finely chopped
1/2 C milk
 grease for deep frying

Combine corn meal and flour; add salt and pepper. Stir in onion,
egg and enough milk to make batter that is not soupy, but can be
dropped from a spoon. Drop mixture by tablespoons into very hot
oil, (400°). Hush puppies will turn themselves over and become
golden brown when done. Drain on paper towels and serve hot.

22 JOHNNY CAKE

1/2 C sugar
1/2 melted shortening or oil
1 egg
1 C sour milk
1 t soda

1/2 t salt
1 C + 2 T flour
1 C yellow cornmeal
1 t baking powder

Combine sugar, shortening and egg. Dissolve soda in milk.
Combine dry ingredients and add to creamed mixture with milk.
Stirring just until mixed. Pour into a greased 8X8 inch pan and
Bake at 425° for 15-20 minutes or until it tests done. 9 servings.

23 CREAMY CORN BREAD OR MUFFINS

1 C flour
1 C cornmeal
1 1/2 T sugar
1 1/2 t baking powder
1/2 t salt

1/2 t soda
2 T butter
2/3 C buttermilk
1 egg
1, 8 oz can creamed style corn

Combine dry ingredients and cut in butter; mix buttermilk, egg and
corn and stir into dry mixture just until blended. Pour into a
greased 8X8 inch pan and bake at 400° for 25-30 minutes or until
it tests done. May also be baked in 12 muffin cups.

24 TEX-MEX CORNBREAD

1 C white corn meal
3/4 t baking soda
1/2 t salt
1/4 C vegetable oil
2 eggs, slightly beaten
1 medium onion, grated

1 C buttermilk
1, 8 oz can creamed style corn
1, 4 oz can green chilies, chopped
1 C grated sharp cheddar cheese

Combine dry ingredients; add oil, eggs, onion, buttermilk, corn and
chilies. Stir until blended. Pour half of batter in a greased heavy
skillet, or an 8X8 inch pan. Sprinkle half the cheese over batter;
pour remaining batter in pan and top with rest of cheese. Bake at
425° for 25 minutes. Serves 6-8.

25 BEER BATTER BREAD

3 1/2 C self-rising flour
1/4 C sugar
1, 12 oz can warm beer
1 egg

Combine flour and sugar; add beer and egg. Stir mixture with a
fork, just until blended. Put batter into a greased bread pan and
bake at 375° for 60-70 minutes or until done. Remove from the
pan and cool on rack. 1 loaf.

26 CHEESE AND POPPY SEED MUFFINS

Low in both fat and calories

3/4 C ricotta cheese
1 egg white, slightly beaten
4 t sugar
1 1/4 C uncooked oatmeal
1/3 C sugar
3 T poppy seed

1 T baking powder
1/2 t grated lemon peel
1/4 t salt
1 C skim milk
3 T oil
2 egg whites, slightly beaten

Mix together cheese, egg white and 4 teaspoons sugar; set aside. Combine all remaining ingredients and mix just until moistened. Spoon 1 tablespoon batter into greased or paper lined muffin cups. Drop 1 tablespoon cheese filling in center of each. Spread remaining batter over filling. Bake at 375° for 20-25 minutes or until lightly browned. Makes 1 dozen.

27 BRAN MUFFINS

These freeze well

3 C all bran cereal
1 C white raisins
1 C boiling water
1 1/2 C flour
3/4-1 C sugar

2 1/2 t soda
1/2 t salt
2 C buttermilk
1/2 C oil
2 eggs

Pour boiling water over cereal and raisins and let cool. Combine flour, sugar, soda, and salt; stir in cereal and raisins, buttermilk, oil and eggs. Stir just until blended, do not beat. Bake in greased muffin tins, at 400° for 12-15 minutes. About 2 dozen muffins.

√To freeze muffins, tip in muffin cups so that air can circulate around them until they are cold. Place muffins on a plate and freeze; when frozen, put in plastic bags.

28 RAISIN BRAN MUFFINS

Store in refrigerator and bake any old time

1 C shortening
3 C sugar
4 eggs
1,15 oz pkg raisin bran cereal
1 qt buttermilk
5 t soda
2 t salt
5 C flour

Cream shortening and sugar; beat in eggs until blended. Combine dry ingredients and add to creamed mixture with cereal and buttermilk. Mix only until blended. Bake as desired and cover remaining batter with foil. Do not stir. Just dip into batter and bake at a later time. Bake muffins at 400° for 15 minutes. (Cold batter will need a little longer baking time.)

29 GINGER BREAD MUFFINS

Also bake as cake for good ginger bread

1 C shortening
1/2 C molasses
1 t cinnamon
2 t ginger
1 C sugar

2 eggs
1/4 t salt
1 t soda
1 C cold water
3 1/4 C flour

Mix together the first six ingredients and beat well. Stir in dry ingredients and mix until blended. Bake at 350° for 20 minutes. Makes 24-30 muffins.

30 BANANA MUFFINS

A favorite in lunch boxes

1 C sugar
4 T shortening
2 eggs
1 C mashed banana

2 C flour
1 t soda
1/4 t salt
1/2 C nut meats

Cream sugar with shortening; beat in eggs. Add banana. Mix well then add dry ingredients and nuts. Stir just until blended. Bake in paper lined muffin cups at 350° for about 20 minutes. Do not over bake. Makes 20 muffins.

31 CRAN-BRAN DIET MUFFINS

Less than 100 calories per muffin

2 C 100 % bran cereal
2 eggs
2 T oil
1 C skim milk

4 T brown sugar
1 C flour
2 t baking powder
2/3 C cranberries, chopped

Combine bran with milk, egg and oil; let stand for 5-10 minutes. Add flour, brown sugar and cranberries and mix just until blended. Spoon mixture into sprayed muffin cups. Bake at 400° for 12-15 minutes or until done. 12 muffins.

32 PINEAPPLE BRAN MUFFINS

2 large eggs
1/2 C brown sugar
1/2 C vegetable oil
1/4 C orange juice (or milk)
1 C bran cereal
1,8 oz can crushed pineapple, undrained

1 t grated orange peel
1 1/2 C flour
2 1/2 t baking powder
1/2 t baking soda
1/2 t salt

Combine eggs, brown sugar, oil, orange juice, crushed pineapple, bran cereal and orange peel. Add dry ingredients alternately with pineapple, stirring just until blended.   Spoon into greased or paper lined muffin cups. Bake at 400° for 20-25 minutes. 12-14 muffins.

33 BLUEBERRY MUFFINS

A good basic recipe; try your own variations*

1-1/2 C flour
1/2 C sugar
2 t baking powder
1/2 t salt

1/4 C soft shortening
1 egg
1/2 C milk
1 C fresh, frozen or canned
    berries

Combine dry ingredients; stir in shortening, egg and milk just until blended. Fold in berries last. Fill greased or paper lined muffin pans 2/3 full. Bake at 400° for 15-20 minutes. Do not overbake.

* Try raisin, date, cherry, dried apricot and more. Follow recipe above omitting blueberries and adding 1 C other fruit, finely chopped Reduce or eliminate sugar with sweeter fruits such as dates and dried apricots and fruits canned in syrup. Bake as directed.

34 RHUBARB BREAD

A moist bread that freezes well

1 1/2 C brown sugar
2/3 C shortening
1 egg
1 C sour milk
1 t salt
1 t soda
1 t vanilla

2 1/2 C flour
1 1/2 C diced rhubarb
1/2 C nuts
Topping:
1 T butter
1/2 C sugar

Cream brown sugar, shortening; add egg and blend. Add combined dry ingredients alternately with milk. Stir in rhubarb and nuts. Pour batter into 2 greased bread pans. Mix topping ingredients and sprinkle over batter. Bake at 325° for 50-60 minutes. Do not overbake.

35 CARAWAY BACON CHEESE BREAD

Serve with salad for a complete lunch

1 1/2 C flour
1/2 C whole wheat flour
1/2 C yellow corn meal
1 1/2 t baking powder
1 t salt
1/2 t baking soda
1 C grated sharp cheddar

1/2 lb bacon
2 t caraway seed
1/4 C oil
2 T sugar
2 egg, slightly beaten
1 1/4 C buttermilk

Fry bacon very crisp; drain on paper towels and crumble.   Mix flours, cornmeal, baking powder, salt and baking soda in large bowl. Add cheese, bacon and caraway seed. Toss with fork to mix. Mix oil, sugar, eggs and buttermilk; add to flour mixture stirring just to blend; do not overmix. Pour into greased bread pan. Bake at 375° for about 40-45 minutes. Makes one loaf.

36 LEMON NUT SURPRISE BREAD

Filling: 1, 8 oz pkg cream cheese
1/3 C sugar
1 egg

Bread:

2 C flour
1/3 C sugar
1/3 C brown sugar, packed
1 t baking soda
1/2 t salt
1/2 C chopped nuts

1/2 C oil
1/2 C milk
2 eggs
1 t grated lemon peel
1/2 t lemon extract

Combine filling ingredients and mix until well blended. Mix dry bread ingredients. Combine oil, milk, eggs, and extract; add to dry ingredients and mix just until blended. Fold in nuts. Put half of batter in a greased 9X5 inch loaf pan. Spread with filling and then with rest of batter. Bake at 350° for 45 minutes. 1 loaf.

37 LEMON BREAD

A delicate taste and texture

1/2 C butter or margarine
1 C sugar
2 eggs, beaten
1 lemon rind, grated
1 1/2 C flour
1 t baking powder

1 t salt
1/2 C milk
1/2 C coconut or walnuts
Topping:
1/4 C sugar
 juice of one lemon

Cream butter and sugar; add eggs and lemon rind. Combine dry
ingredients and add to creamed mixture alternately with milk. Stir
in coconut or nuts. Bake in a loaf pan at 350° for 50 minutes.
Before removing from pan, poke shallow holes in top of loaf and
pour topping over bread. Let stand 20 minutes, then remove from
pan. 1 loaf.

38 TIN CAN RAISIN BREAD

Wrap in Christmas foil for last minute gifts

2 C sugar
2 eggs
4 T shortening
2 t vanilla
1, 1 lb box dark seedless raisins

3 C boiling water
5 1/2 C flour
3 t soda
1/2 t salt
1 cup nut meats

Pour boiling water over raisins and let cool. Cream sugar and shortening until blended; add eggs and vanilla. add flour to creamed mixture with raisins. Stir in nut meats. Bake bread in 1 pound tin vegetable cans. Wash, dry and spray cans well with cooking spray. Fill cans 1/2 -2/3 full. Bake at 350° for 45 -60 minutes or until loaves test done with a tooth pick. Let stand in cans until cool. Tip loaves out of cans and wrap in foil. Bread freezes well.

39 CARROT BREAD

Bake in bread pan, or in tin cans for moist round slices

2 C flour
2 t soda
2 t cinnamon
1/2 t salt
1 1/3 C sugar
1/2 C currants

1/2 C chopped pecans
2/3 C oil
2 t vanilla
3 eggs
2 C grated carrots

Combine dry ingredients and stir in currants and nuts. Stir in remaining ingredients and stir just until blended. Pour into one greased bread pan or into three greased #2 size cans. Bake at 350° for 1 hour, or less for tin cans. Cool slightly and remove from pan or cans. Cool, wrap in plastic wrap and refrigerate to store.

√Freeze half loaves, or put plastic wrap between halves so that you don't have to thaw whole loaves.

40 PRUNE GRAHAM BREAD

An old fashioned recipe

1 1/2 C all-purpose flour
1 C whole wheat flour
1 t baking soda
1/2 t salt
1 large egg

1/4 C sugar
1/2 C molasses
3/4 C buttermilk
1/4 C butter, melted
1/2 C chopped prunes

Stir together the flours, baking soda and salt. Beat egg, add sugar and molasses and beat until blended. Add the flour mixture, buttermilk, butter and prunes; stir until the flour mixture is moistened. Turn into a greased loaf pan and bake at 350° for about 45 minutes. (Top of bread will be cracked). Loosen edges and turn out to cool on a wire rack. 1 loaf.

41 PEANUT BUTTER BREAD

1 1/2 flour
1 C sugar
1 T baking powder
1/2 t salt

1/2 C chunk style peanut butter
1 C quick or old fashioned oats
1 egg, beaten
1 C milk

Combine flour, sugar, baking powder and salt; cut in peanut butter until mixture resembles coarse meal. Stir in oats, milk and egg. Stir just until blended. Pour batter into greased bread pan and bake at 350° for 1 hour.

42 PEANUT BREAD

2 3/4 C whole wheat flour
3/4 C brown sugar
3 1/2 t baking powder
1 t salt

1 1/2 C milk
1/2 C peanut butter
1 egg
1/2 C chopped peanuts

Mix all ingredients in order given. Pour batter into a greased bread pan and bake at 350° for 55-60 minutes. Test for doneness with a toothpick. Cool on rack. Chill for easier slicing.

43 PUMPKIN BREAD

After the Jack O' Lantern...

2 2/3 C sugar
4 eggs
2/3 C shortening
2 C pumpkin
3 1/3 C flour
1 1/2 t salt

1/2 t baking powder
2 t cinnamon
1/2 t cloves
2/3 C water
2/3 C nuts
2/3 C raisins or dates

Combine sugar, eggs, shortening and pumpkin. Stir dry ingredients together and add to creamed mixture alternately with water. Stir in nuts and fruit. Fill greased tin cans 1/2-2/3 full and bake at 350° for 1 hour.

44 CHERRY NUT BREAD

With maraschino cherries; a pretty Christmas bread

1 C sugar
1/2 C shortening
2 eggs
2 1/4 C flour
2 t baking powder

1/2 t salt
1/2 C milk
1/4 C maraschino cherry juice
3/4 C chopped pecans
1/3 C cut up maraschino cherries

Cream sugar, shortening and eggs until light. Stir baking powder
and salt into flour. Add dry ingredients to creamed mixture
alternately with milk and cherry juice, stirring just until moistened.
Fold in cherries and nuts. Bake in a greased 9X5X3 inch loaf pan
at 350° 35-45 minutes or until it tests done. Turn out of pan, cool
and wrap in foil.

45   PINEAPPLE ZUCCHINI BREAD

A very moist, luscious loaf

3 eggs
2 C sugar
2/3 C oil
2 t vanilla
2 C zucchini, shredded
1, 8 1/4 oz can crushed pineapple
3 C flour

1 1/2 t cinnamon
1 t salt
2 t baking soda
1/4 t baking powder
3/4 t nutmeg
1 C chopped nuts
1 C raisins

Cream eggs, sugar, oil and vanilla; zucchini and drained pine-apple. Stir dry ingredients together and add to creamed mixture. Stir in nuts and raisins. Grease and flour 2 bread pans. Fill pans 2/3 full. Bake at 350° for 1 hour. 2 loaves.

46 APPLE BREAD

Macintosh apples are best for bread.

3/4 C margarine
1 C white sugar
3 eggs
1 t vanilla
3 C flour
1 t salt
1 t soda

1/2 C chopped nuts
3 T buttermilk
3 C diced, unpeeled apple
Topping:
3 T brown sugar
1 T flour
2 t cinnamon

Cream together margarine, sugar, eggs, and vanilla; Combine dry ingredients and add to creamed mixture with fruits, nuts and milk. Fill pans 2/3 full. Blend topping ingredients and sprinkle over batter. Bake at 350° for 45 minutes. Makes 2 loaves.

47 DIABETIC ORANGE DATE BREAD

Plenty sweet without sugar

1/2 C margarine
4 eggs, beaten
1 C orange juice
1 C water
4 t sucaryl solution
2 t baking powder

4 C flour
1 t baking soda
1 t salt
1/2 C chopped pecans
20 dates cut in pieces
2 t grated orange rind

Cream margarine and add eggs, orange juice, water, and sucaryl solution. Combine dry ingredients and add to creamed mixture mixing until blended. Pour into two greased loaf pans and let stand twenty minutes before baking. Bake in a 350° oven for 55 minutes. 2 loaves.

48 CRANBERRY ORANGE BREAD

A pretty party bread for the holidays

2 C flour
1 C sugar
1 T grated orange peel
1 1/2 t baking powder
1 t salt
1/2 t soda

3/4 C orange juice
2 T butter, melted
1 egg
1 C chopped cranberries
1/2 C chopped nuts

Combine all ingredients except cranberries and nuts; mix well. Stir in cranberries and nuts. Pour into greased or sprayed bundt pan or ring mold. Bake at 350° for 35-45 min or until toothpick inserted in center comes out clean. Remove immediately from pan. Serve warm or cool. 1 loaf.

49 MASHED POTATO FRIED CAKES

These stay moist and soft; good plain or sugar coated

1/4 C melted margarine
1 1/3 C sugar
1 C mashed potato
2 eggs, beaten
4 C *sifted* flour
5 t baking powder
1 t salt
1 t nutmeg
1/2 C milk

Cream margarine, sugar, eggs and potatoes until blended. Combine dry ingredients and add to creamed ingredients alternately with milk. Cover batter tightly with foil or plastic wrap and chill for several hours or overnight. Turn batter on to a floured board and roll or pat to a thickness of 1/2 to 1/3 inch. Cut with a floured cutter. Fry in hot oil at 375° for about 1 minute on each side. 3 dozen fried cakes.

50 BLUEBERRY TEA CAKE

From Muskegon, Michigan where blueberries grow

1/4 C shortening
1 C sugar
1 egg
2 C flour
2 t baking powder

1/4 t salt
3/4 C milk
1 t vanilla
3 C blueberries, fresh or frozen

Topping:
1/4 C sugar
1/3 C flour

1/2 t cinnamon
2 1/2 T butter

Cream shortening and sugar; add egg and beat until light and fluffy. Sift dry ingredients and add to creamed mixture alternately with milk and vanilla. Fold in blueberries. Pour into a 9 inch square pan. Combine topping ingredients until crumbly and sprinkle over raw batter. Bake at 350° for 45-50 minutes.

51 SOUR CREAM COFFEE CAKE

A rich, tender brunch favorite

1/2 C shortening
3/4 C sugar
1 t vanilla
3 eggs

2 C flour
1 t baking powder
1 t baking soda
1 C sour cream

*Topping:**
6 T butter
1 C brown sugar

2 t cinnamon
1 C nuts

Cream shortening and sugar; add eggs and vanilla and blend well. Combine dry ingredients and mix into batter with sour cream. Spread half of batter in greased and floured tube pan. Combine topping ingredients until crumbly. Spread half of topping over batter in pan. Cover with remaining batter and then with rest of topping. Bake at 350° for 50 minutes. Serves 12.

***Variation:** Spread half of batter in a 9X13 pan; top with 1, 1 lb 5 oz can pie filling; cherry, raisin, peach, apple etc. Combine 1/2 C sugar and 1 t cinnamon. Sprinkle filling with half of sugar-spice mixture, pour on rest of batter and sprinkle with remaining sugar. Bake as above.

52 CHERRY ALMOND COFFEE CAKE

Serves a big crowd for breakfast

1 1/2 C sugar
1 C butter or margarine
2 eggs
1 t vanilla
1 C milk
1 t almond extract
3 C flour
1 t baking powder
1/2 t salt
1 1/2 cans cherry pie filling

Glaze:
1 C confectioners sugar
1/2 t almond extract
1 1/2 T milk

Cream sugar and butter; add eggs, beating well. Add vanilla and almond extract. Mix flour, baking powder and salt; add to creamed mixture alternately with milk. Spread two-thirds of mixture on a greased 10X15 jelly roll pan. Spread pie filling evenly over batter. Drop remaining batter by spoonsful on cherries. Bake at 350° for 25-30 minutes. Cool slightly and drizzle glaze over the top. Serve warm. Serves 12.

√ **See also quicker breads and yeast breads for more coffee cakes.**

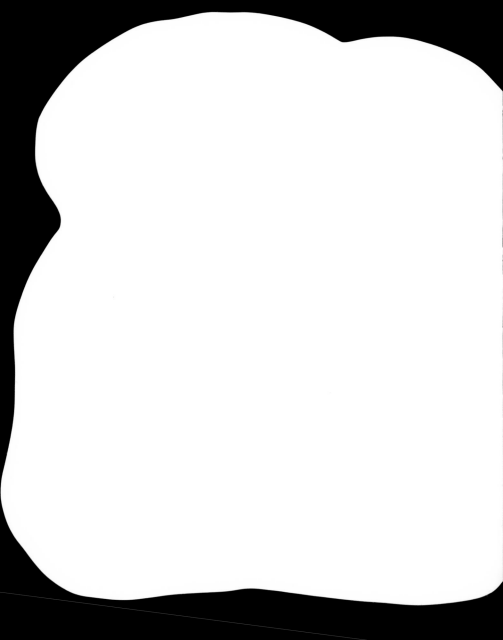

QUICKER BREADS, MIXES & SHORTCUTS

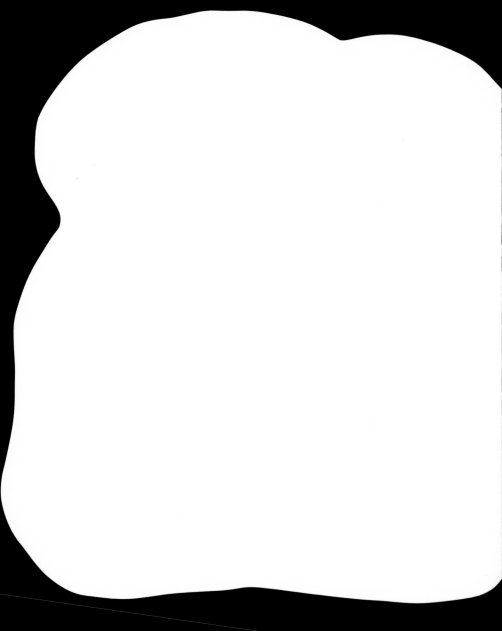

53   EASY BREAD STICKS

1 pkg hot dog buns
1 stick butter or margarine   parsley
garlic, minced or put through press   Parmesan cheese
                                       paprika

Cut buns in quarters and place on cookie sheet, bread side up. Melt butter and mix in garlic and parsley to taste. Brush butter on buns with a pastry brush. Sprinkle with Parmesan cheese and paprika. Bake at 300° until crisp and golden. Makes 32 sticks.

54   SPAGHETTI CHEESE STICKS

Make these in a minute with leftover buns

Leftover hamburg or hot dog buns. Spread pieces lightly with margarine and sprinkle with Parmesan cheese, garlic salt, paprika or other seasoning of choice. Broil for just a minute or two at serving time.

55 QUICK SKILLET BISCUITS

1 tube refrigerator biscuits
butter

Preheat fry pan or electric skillet. Grease lightly with butter. Place biscuits in pan. Cover and bake for three minutes. Turn biscuits over and continue baking three to four minutes, or until nicely browned. Serve with jelly or marmalade. 10 biscuits.

56 BROCCOLI CORN BREAD

1/4 C margarine
1 C cooked, chopped broccoli
1, 8 1/2 oz pkg corn muffin mix
2 eggs
1 C cottage cheese
3 T chopped onion

Melt margarine in a 8X8 inch pan. Combine all other ingredients and pour batter over melted margarine. Bake at 375° for 20-25 minutes or until lightly browned. Do not underbake.

57 NEVER FAIL TURKEY STUFFING

*Vary the basic recipe to your family's taste**

1 loaf bread
2 C water
1/2 C margarine
1 envelope dry onion soup mix
2 t sage or poultry seasoning

Melt margarine in water; add soup mix and stir to dissolve. Tear bread into small pieces and sprinkle seasoning over it. Pour liquid over bread and stir to mix, then mix with hands. Stuff bird, or bake stuffing in a separate greased pan. If you like very moist dressing, add chicken or turkey broth until mixture is very wet, or spoon stuffing directly into pan juices around bird during last 45 minutes of roasting time.

* Substituting some dry croutons for some of the bread changes the texture.
*Adding 1/2 C.mashed potato adds moisture to the dressing.
*Saute some celery and/or mushrooms in some of the margarine and add to the bread.

58 CORN BREAD DRESSING

2 T margarine
1 small onion, chopped
1 stalk celery, chopped
3 C corn bread
2 C bread crumbs
3 eggs
1/2 t pepper
1 1/2 t sage
4 C chicken broth
1 C cream of chicken soup

Cook onion and celery in margarine until soft. Combine onions, and celery, breads, eggs and seasonings. Heat chicken soup and broth together until soup is dissolved; pour broth over bread mixture and mix with a fork. Bake covered at 350° for 35-45 minutes. Serves 12-15.

59 EGGS IN A BREAD BASKET

Try this for a holiday breakfast for a crowd

1 loaf French or Italian bread
butter-flavored cooking spray
8-10 eggs
1 C shredded cheese

Cut off top of loaf bread. Remove the insides of the bread* leaving a 1 inch shell all around. Spray inside of hollowed loaf with butter flavored cooking spray. Place loaf on a baking sheet and bake at 350° for 8-10 minutes. (Bread may be prepared ahead then baked while the rest of breakfast is cooking.) Prepare scrambled eggs with ham, bacon, and seasonings of choice. Spoon eggs lightly into bread shell and top with cheese. Broil for 2-3 minutes to melt cheese. Serve whole loaf at the table and cut in slices appropriate to size of guests.

*Use the scooped-out bread to stuff the bird.

60 BREAKFAST PIZZA I

A gourmet breakfast in just minutes

1 loaf frozen bread dough, thawed
5-6 eggs, scrambled and cooled
1 1/2 C fresh or canned mushrooms, sliced
1/2 C chopped green pepper
2 T chopped onion
1 C chopped, cooked ham, bacon or sausage
1 1/4 C shredded cheddar cheese
1/2 C shredded Swiss or mozzarella cheese

Roll out dough to fit a large greased pizza pan or cookie sheet. Spread all other ingredients over dough in order given.* (Can make ahead and refrigerate at this point.) Bake at 450-475° for 6-8 minutes or until crust is done and cheeses are melted. Serves 6.

61   BREAKFAST PIZZA II

1, 8 oz pkg pizza crust mix or 1 pkg crescent refrigerator rolls
1 lb bulk pork sausage
1 C frozen hash brown potatoes, thawed
1 C shredded cheese
4 eggs
3 T milk
salt and pepper to taste
2 T Parmesan cheese

Prepare crust mix as directed and pat onto a greased pizza pan,
or separate crescent rolls and press onto pan.   Cook sausage,
drain well, cool and spoon over crust. Sprinkle potatoes and
cheese over crust. Beat eggs, milk, salt and pepper together and
pour over crust. Sprinkle with Parmesan cheese. Bake at 375° for
30 minutes or until eggs are set and crust is brown. Serves 6-8.

62 QUICK MIX

Make-your-own biscuit mix

8 1/2 C flour
1 T baking powder
1 T salt
2 t cream of tartar

1 t baking soda
1 1/2 C dry milk
2 1/4 C vegetable shortening

Stir dry ingredients together; cut in shortening with pastry blender until mixture is the texture of cornmeal. Store in an airtight container in a cool place. Use within 3 months. 13 cups mix.

63 QUICK MIX PANCAKES

1 C quick mix   3/4 C milk

Mix until blended and bake on a hot skillet.

64 QUICK MIX WAFFLES

2 C quick mix   2 eggs
1 1/4 C milk   2 T oil

Blend ingredients and bake on a hot waffle iron.

65 QUICK MIX DUMPLINGS

2 C quick mix   2 eggs
1 1/4 C milk   2 T oil

Blend ingredients and drop into boiling soup or stew. Sprinkle with
parsley, turn to simmer and cook, covered for 12-15 minutes.

66 QUICK APPLESAUCE FRIED CAKES

2 C quick mix   1/2 C apple sauce
2 T sugar   2 t cinnamon
1 egg   1 t vanilla

Combine ingredients and mix until smooth. Chill for 2 hours. Turn
dough onto a floured board and roll to 1/2 inch thick. Cut with a
floured cutter and fry in oil at 375° for about 1/2 minute on each
side. Drain on paper towels and roll in powdered sugar.

BREAD MACHINERY

Bread machines come in two sizes and several styles. Basically, they do the mixing, kneading, raising and baking for you, with the end product being one round loaf. Various models differ in degree of automation. Here, the left column shows the measurments for the smaller machine. Right column for the larger. Always use the method recommended with your machine.

67 DILLY ONION BREAD

1/2 pkg dry yeast	1 pkg dry yeast
2 C flour	3 C flour
2 t sugar	1 T sugar
3/4 t salt	1 t salt
1 egg	1 egg
2 t prepared mustard	1 T prepared mustard
2 T instant minced onion	3 T instant minced onion
1 T dill seed	2 T dill seed
2 t oil	1 T oil
1 C milk	1 1/4 C milk

√1 pkg dry yeast contains 2 teaspoons yeast. Yeast can be purchased in bulk.

68 BREAD MACHINE MANY GRAINS BREAD

1 1/2 t dry yeast
3/4 C white flour
3/4 C whole wheat flour
3/4 t salt
1/4 C rye flour
1/4 C corn meal
1/4 C quick oatmeal
1 T sunflower seed
3/4 t poppy seed
1 T dark molasses
3/4 T oil
1 C water

1 pkg dry yeast
1 C white flour
1 C whole wheat flour
1 t salt
1/4 C rye flour
1/4 C corn meal
1/2 C quick oatmeal
1 1/2 T sunflower seed
1 t poppy seed
1 1/2 T dark molasses
1 T oil
1 1/4 C water

√Try soy flour in place of cornmeal or other flours.

BREAD MACHINE
CALIFORNIA SOUR DOUGH

1/3 C sourdough starter	1/2 C sourdough starter
1 t dry yeast	1 pkg dry yeast
2 C + 2 T white flour	3 C flour
3/4 t salt	1 t salt
3/4 t sugar	1 t sugar
1/4 t soda	1/4 t soda
2/3 C water	3/4 C water

√SOUR DOUGH STARTER

1pkg dry yeast	2 C flour
21/2 C warm water	1 T sugar or honey

Dissolve yeast in 1/2 C water; add rest of ingredients and beat until smooth. Pour into large glass jar and cover with cheese cloth. Let stand at room temperature for 5-10 days until fermented, stirring 2-3 times a day. Store in refrigerator, still covered with cheese cloth. Feed starter 1 teaspoon sugar every 10 days. To replentish starter, stir 3/4 C each flour and water, and 1 teaspoon sugar into remaining amount. Let stand at room temperature for 1 day.

70 BRUNCH COFFEE CAKE

You'll make this often! Change the flavors with the mixes

1 pkg yellow cake mix
1 pkg instant vanilla pudding mix
1 pkg instant butterscotch pudding mix
2/3 C oil
1 C water
4 eggs

Topping:
1 1/2 C brown sugar
1 T cinnamon
2/3 C nuts

Combine mixes with oil, water and eggs and blend. Pour 1/2 of batter into a greased 13X9 inch cake pan. Stir topping ingredients together and sprinkle half of mixture over batter in pan. Pour rest of batter into pan, and top with rest of topping. Bake at 325° for 55-60 minutes.

71 FROZEN DOUGH MONKEY BUNS

2 loaves frozen bread dough or 20 frozen rolls (Do not thaw)
1 pkg butterscotch pudding mix (not instant)
1/2 C butter
1/2-1 C brown sugar
2 T cinnamon
1 C nuts

Cut up frozen dough into 1 inch pieces. Place in a well greased
angel food cake pan. Drizzle butter over dough. Sprinkle dry
ingredients and nuts over dough. Put pan in cold oven and leave
over night. In the morning, turn oven to 350° and bake for 25-30
minutes. Invert buns on waxed paper.

72 CHOCOLATE BREAD PUDDING

So pretty with meringue

5-6 slices stale bread
1/4 C margarine
2 eggs, separated
2 C milk
3 T cocoa
1/2 t salt
1/3 C packed brown sugar
1 t vanilla
4 T sugar

Spread bread with margarine and cut into squares. Place bread in a well greased 1 1/2 quart casserole. Stir milk into cocoa to make a thin paste. Add paste to remaining milk. Beat egg yolks until light; add milk and blend. Stir in salt, sugar and vanilla. Pour liquid over bread in casserole. Bake at 350° for 45-50 minutes. Beat egg whites until stiff and beat in 4 tablespoons sugar. Spread meringue over baked pudding and return to oven until browned. Serves 6.

73 LOUISIANA BREAD PUDDING

Try this for your next party!

1 loaf stale French bread
8 T butter, melted
2 C sugar
2 T C vanilla
1 t nutmeg

1 t cinnamon
1 C coconut
1 C raisins
1 C chopped pecans
4 C milk

Crumble French bread. There should be 6-8 cups. Combine bread with all other ingredients. Mixture should be quite moist, but not soupy. Pour mixture in a greased 9X13 baking pan. Place in a cold oven and turn oven to 350°. Bake for 1 1/4 hours or until top is golden and knife inserted in mixture comes out clean.

Whiskey sauce:

1/2 C butter
1 1/2 C powdered sugar
2 egg yolks
1/2 C bourbon whiskey, or other liquor to taste (or fruit juice if preferred)

Heat butter and sugar until combined. Remove from heat and blend in egg yolks. Add liquor or juice to taste. Serve warm over warm pudding. Serves 20.

YEAST BREADS,
BUNS
& SWEET ROLLS

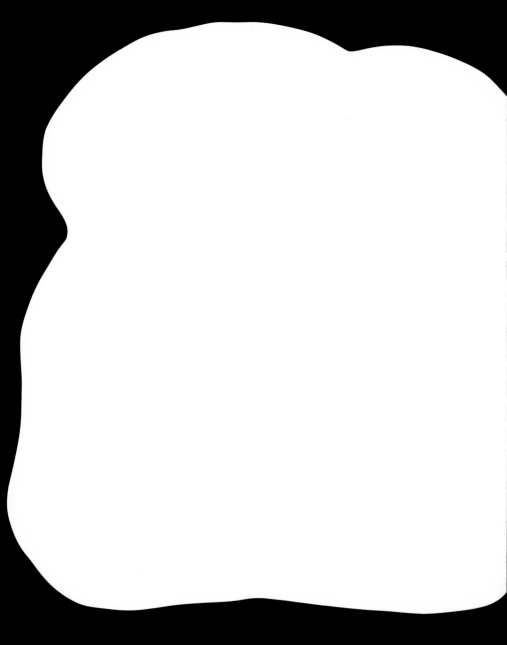

74 Fresh Potato Bread

Potatoes encourage yeast to rise

1 medium potato
2 C water
2 pkg dry yeast
1/2 C lukewarm water
3 T sugar

1 T salt
1/3 C dry milk
3 T shortening
6 1/2 C flour (about)

Cook potato until done in the 2 cups water. Mash potato in the water and add more liquid if needed to make 2 1/2 cups. Dissolve yeast in 1/2 C warm water. Combine sugar, salt, shortening and dry milk with potato water. Cool to lukewarm, stir in yeast and 2 cups flour; beat until smooth. Stir in remaining flour, turn out on floured board and knead until smooth and elastic. Place in a greased bowl and turn dough to grease top; let rise until double. Punch dough down and let rise again. Shape dough into two loaves and place in greased loaf pans. Cover and let rise. Bake at 350° for 35-40 minutes.

75 WHITE BREAD

A starting point for many family favorites

2 1/2 C warm water
2 pkg active dry yeast
1/2 C instant nonfat dry milk
2 T sugar
2 t salt
1/3 C cooking oil or shortening
7 to 7 1/2 C all purpose flour

Sprinkle yeast over warm water into large mixer bowl. Add dry milk, sugar, salt, oil and about 3 C flour. Beat for 3 minutes with a mixer. Gradually stir in remaining flour by hand to form a very stiff dough. Turn dough onto a floured surface and knead until smooth. Divide in half and shape dough into a 12x6 inch rectangle.* Roll up tightly, starting with 6 inch side. Seal edges and ends. Place, seam side down, in greased bread pans. Makes 2 loaves.

To bake the same day: Cover; let rise in warm place until doubled in size, about 1 hour. Bake at 375° for 35-40 minutes. Remove from pans immediately and brush with butter. Cool on a wire rack.

To bake later: Place bread pans in large plastic bags, allowing enough room for bread to rise, and refrigerate several hours or overnight. Prick any air bubbles on surface. Bake at 375° for 35-40 min. Remove from pans immediately and brush with butter. Cool on wire racks.

76 RAISIN, CINNAMON, RAISIN CINNAMON BREAD

To make raisin bread, stir 1/2 C raisins or currants *per loaf* into dough with the remaining flour *or,* while shaping dough, press the raisins into the dough before rolling into the loaf.

To make cinnamon bread, combine 1/4 C white sugar and 1 1/2 teaspoon cinnamon *per loaf* and spread over rectangle before rolling into loaf. To make raisin-cinnamon bread, sprinkle 1/3 C raisins over cinnamon-sugar mixture and press into dough before rolling loaf.

√ Both raisin and cinnamon loaves may be frosted with powdered sugar icing unless you plan to toast bread.

77 PINWHEEL BREAD

White and whole wheat dough rolled together

1 pkg dry yeast
1/4 C warm water
2 C milk
2 T sugar
2 T shortening or oil

2 t salt
3-5 C white flour
2 C whole wheat flour

Dissolve yeast in water. Heat milk just to boiling point. Combine sugar, shortening and salt; stir in milk and cool to lukewarm. Divide liquid mixture, stirring 2-3 C white flour into one half, and wheat flour into other half. Knead each portion separately on floured board until smooth. Shape into 2 balls and raise in greased bowls until double. Punch down both white and whole wheat balls, *divide each one in half* and let rest 10 minutes. To form loaves: Roll one whole wheat ball to 8X16 inch rectangle. Repeat with one white ball. Place white rectangle on top of whole wheat. Starting at narrow end, roll up jelly-roll fashion. Seal edges by pressing down firmly. Place in greased bread pans, sealed-side down. Lightly brush tops with butter or margarine. Let rise in warm place until doubled. Bake at 400° for 35-40 minutes or until golden brown.   Immediately remove from pans and brush with butter or margarine. Cool on wire rack. Makes 2, 1 lb loaves.

78 HONEY WHOLE WHEAT BREAD

Five delicious loaves

5 C warm water
2 pkg dry yeast
1/2 C dry milk powder*
1/4 C honey
4 C whole wheat flour

1/2 C instant mashed potatoes**
6 T oil
1 T salt
6 1/2-8 C white flour

Combine water, yeast, milk powder, honey, whole wheat flour, instant potato flakes, oil, salt and half of white flour. Beat for 2 minutes with mixer until smooth. Stir in remaining white flour and turn onto a floured board. Knead until light and elastic. Let raise until doubled in bulk. Punch down and let rest for 5 minutes. Make into 5 loaves, place in greased pans and let raise. Bake at 375° for 35-45 minutes.

*Or substitute 1 1/2 C liquid milk for same amount of water in recipe.
**Or substitute 1 cup mashed potato.

79 SWEDISH RYE BREAD

A touch of orange flavor in these lovely loaves

2 C milk
2/3 C oil
2 pkg dry yeast
1 t sugar
1 C lukewarm water
1 t salt

1 1/3 C dark corn syrup
7-8 C white flour
2 C rye flour
1 orange rind, grated

Scald milk and pour into mixing bowl to cool. Add oil. Dissolve
yeast and sugar in water. When milk is lukewarm, add salt, corn
syrup, 3 C white flour, 2 C rye flour, yeast mixture, and grated
orange rind. Beat until smooth with mixer. Stir in remaining white
flour, beating in as much as possible with mixer, then adding the
rest by hand. Turn out on floured board and knead for 10 minutes
or until the dough feels smooth and satiny. Place in large greased
bowl, and allow to rise until double in bulk. Shape dough into 4
loaves, place in bread pans and allow to rise again until double.
Bake at 350° for about 40 minutes. Makes 4 loaves.

80 CARAWAY RYE BREAD

Only needs to rise once

3 C warm water
1 pkg dry yeast
1 T sugar
1 T salt
2 T caraway seed
2 T butter
1 C medium rye flour
8-9 C white flour

Combine warm water, yeast, butter, sugar and salt, stirring to dissolve. Stir in rye flour and caraway seed; let stand for 5-10 minutes until mixture starts to bubble. Stir in white flour and turn out onto floured board. Knead until very smooth and elastic. Divide into 2 or 3 loaves, again kneading each piece well. Place loaves in greased bread pans, butter tops and let rise. Bake at 375° for 35-40 minutes. 2 large loaves.

81 SUNFLOWER LOAF

1 1/4 C warm water
1 pkg active dry yeast
2 t sugar
1/4 C honey
1/2 C buttermilk
1 1/2 t salt, if desired

4 C whole wheat flour
1/2 C toasted sunflower seeds
1/2 C untoasted sunflower seeds
1 egg yolk
1 T milk

Dissolve the yeast and sugar in warm water. Add the honey, buttermilk and salt, four cups of flour and 1/2 C of toasted sunflower seeds, mixing well. Turn the dough out onto a lightly floured board and knead it for about 10 minutes. (The dough will be sticky until after it rises.) Shape dough into a ball. Coat the dough lightly with flour and place it on a baking sheet. Cover with plastic wrap and let rise in a warm place for 20 minutes. Knead the dough again and form into a ball. Let the dough rise, covered, a second time for about 40 minutes. Shape into a loaf and place in greased loaf pan. Mix egg yolk and milk and brush the loaf with egg mixture. Sprinkle 1/2 C of untoasted sunflower seeds over loaf and press seeds into bread. Cover the pan with plastic wrap and let it rise for 45 minutes. Bake at 375° for about 40 minutes. Makes 2 small or 1 large loaf.

82 ED'S BREAD

Never did meet Ed, but do love his bread!

2 C milk
3/4 C water
4 T margarine
2/3 C cornmeal

1 T molasses
2 pkg dry yeast
5-6 C flour

Bring milk, water, margarine, and cornmeal to a boil and let cool.
When mixture is lukewarm, add molasses, yeast and 1 cup flour;
beat with a mixer for 2 minutes. Stir in part of remaining flour and
turn onto a floured board. Knead until light and elastic. Place in a
greased bowl and let rise for 45 minutes. Make into 2 loaves. Let
rise until double in bulk. Bake at 350° for 50-55 minutes or until
done.

√ After kneading, top of dough should be greased while it is rising
to prevent dough from drying out. A quick way to do this is to
grease bowl, turn dough around once in bowl and turn greased
side up. Cover with a towel.

83 HONEY OAT BREAD

1 C boiling water
1-1/2 C rolled oats
1/3 C honey
1/4 C butter
3 t salt

1 C dairy sour cream
2 pkgs dry yeast
1/2 C warm water
2 eggs
6-61/2 C flour

Combine boiling water, oats, honey, butter and salt. Stir until butter is melted. Add sour cream and cool to lukewarm. Soften yeast in water, stir in eggs and 2 C flour; add to oat mixture and beat until smooth. Stir in additional flour to make stiff dough. Turn onto floured board and knead until elastic. Let dough rest 20 minutes. Shape into two loaves and place in greased bread pans. Cover loosely with plastic wrap and refrigerate 2-24 hours. When ready to bake, remove from refrigerator and let stand at room temperature for 10 minutes. Bake at 375° for 40-45 minutes. 2 loaves.

84 OATMEAL BREAD

Four flavorful loaves

1 C whole wheat flour
1/4 C shortening
2 T salt
1 C brown sugar
1/3 C molasses

2 C oatmeal
4 C boiling water
3 pkg dry yeast
1 C warm water
10 C white flour

Combine wheat flour, shortening, salt, brown sugar, molasses, oatmeal and boiling water. Stir until mixed. Dissolve yeast in warm water and add to other ingredients. Stir in as much white flour as possible and turn dough onto a floured board. Knead until smooth. Place in a greased bowl and let rise until double. Form into loaves, place in greased bread pans and let rise until double. Bake at 350° for 30-40 minutes. 4 large loaves.

√ If a plastic bowl or container is used for raising dough, it need not be greased; however top of dough will need greasing. Cooking spray works fine for this.

85   HEALTH BREAD

Positively bulging with healthy ingredients

8 1/2 C flour
3/4 C dry milk
2 t salt
1 pkg dry yeast
2 2/3 C water

1 C plain yogurt
4 T honey
1 T margarine
1 C wheat germ
1 egg

Combine 4 cups flour (white flour or a combination of whole wheat and white), dry milk, salt and yeast in a large mixer bowl. Mix water, yogurt, honey and margarine in a sauce pan and heat until margarine is melted. Pour warm mixture into flour and beat with a mixer for about 2 minutes. Stir in wheat germ and additional flour, one cup at a time until a stiff dough is formed. Turn dough onto a floured board and knead until smooth and elastic. Place dough in a greased bowl and turn dough over so that top is greased. Cover and let rise until doubled in bulk. Punch down, shape into a loaf, and place in a greased bread pan. Cover and let rise until doubled. Brush loaf with beaten egg and sprinkle with wheat germ. Bake at 350° for about 35 minutes.

86 TOMATO BREAD

Pretty, tasty round loaves

1 pkg active dry yeast
1/4 C warm water
2 T sugar
1/2 C warm milk
1/4 C butter or margarine
1 egg

1 t nutmeg
1 t salt
1 1/2 t Italian seasoning
1, 12 oz can tomato paste
2 1/2 C whole wheat flour
3 C white flour

Dissolve yeast in warm water; add sugar and let stand for 15 minutes. Add all other ingredients including whole wheat flour and about 1/2 C white flour. Beat with a mixer until blended. Stir in as much white flour as possible and turn out onto a floured board. Knead until smooth. Place dough in a greased bowl and turn to grease top of loaf. Cover with plastic wrap and let rise until double. Punch down and divide dough in half. Knead each loaf briefly and shape into a ball. Place on a greased baking sheet and flatten slightly. Slash tops of loaves, cover and let rise until almost double. Bake at 350° for 30 to 40 minutes. Cool on racks.
  Two round loaves.

87   PEASANT BREAD

No kneading; rather flat, but delicious loaves

2 C water, lukewarm
1 pkg dry yeast
1 T sugar
2 t salt

4 C flour
2 T cornmeal
melted butter

Combine water, yeast, sugar and salt and mix until dissolved. Stir in flour until blended. Place mixture (without kneading) in a greased bowl. Cover with a damp cloth. Let raise 45 minutes or until doubled. Grease a baking sheet and sprinkle with cornmeal. Divide dough into 2 parts, shaping into oblong loaves and place on sheet. Let raise 45 minutes. Brush loaves with melted butter. Bake at 425° for 10 minutes, then at 375° for 20 minutes. Brush loaves again with butter and serve.

√ Dough that is not kneaded, or raised only once, such as batter breads will produce a coarser finished loaf. These breads are best served warm from the oven.

88 OVER NIGHT FRENCH BREAD

Make the dough and bake whenever

7 1/2 C flour (about)
2 T sugar
1 T salt
1 pkg quick rise yeast
2 1/2 C hot water

Mix 6 1/2 cups of flour with yeast, sugar and salt. Stir hot water
into flour mixture and turned out on floured board, mixing in
enough additional flour to make a soft dough. Knead well for 8-10
minutes. Put dough into a greased bowl and cover tightly with
plastic wrap. Refrigerate for 1-2 days. When ready to bake, punch
down dough and divide in half. Form each half into a long loaf.
Place on greased cookie sheets. Make deep slashes across
loaves. Let rise until doubled in size. Brush loaves lightly with
water and Bake at 400° for 25-30 minutes.

89 INDIAN RYE BATTER BREAD

2 C white flour
3/4 C cornmeal
1 pkg dry yeast
1 C milk
1/4 C molasses
2 T shortening
1/4 C water
1 t salt
3/4 C rye flour

Mix 1 1/2 C white flour, cornmeal and yeast in a mixer bowl. Heat milk, molasses, shortening, water and salt just until shortening is melted. Add liquid to flour mixture and beat for three minutes. Stir in rye flour and remaining white flour. Do not knead. Cover and let rise until double in bulk. Stir down and place batter in a greased 1 1/2 quart casserole dish. Cover and let rise again until almost double. Bake at 325° for 30 minutes. Cover top of bread with foil and bake 20 minutes more. Remove from dish and cool on a rack. Makes 1 round loaf.

90 DILLY CHEESE BATTER BREAD

1 pkg dry yeast
1/4 C warm water
1 C small curd cottage cheese
    (heated to lukewarm)
2 T instant minced onion
1 T butter

2 t dill seed
1 t salt
1/4 t soda
1 unbeaten egg
2-21/2 C flour
garlic butter

Dissolve yeast in water. Combine cottage cheese, sugar, onion, butter, dill seed, salt, soda, and egg; add yeast mixture and beat until blended. Add flour and beat until it forms a stiff dough. Cover and let rise until double in bulk, 50-60 minutes. Stir down and turn into a well-greased tube pan. Let rise 30-40 minutes. Bake in 350° oven for 40 minutes. Remove from oven and brush with garlic butter. Cool and slice. To serve warm, wrap in foil and reheat in slow oven until heated through.

91 SOURDOUGH BREAD

1 C sourdough starter*
1 pkg dry yeast
1 1/2 C warm water
5 1/2-6 C flour

2 t salt
2 t sugar
1/2 t soda

Dissolve yeast in water; stir in 2 1/2 cups flour, salt, sugar, and sourdough starter. Combine soda with 2 1/2 cups flour and stir into mixture. Stir in as much more flour as possible and turn dough onto a floured board. Knead until smooth, place in a greased bowl and let rise until double, about 1- 1/2 hours. Punch down and let rest for 10 minutes. Shape into two 9 inch loaves on a greased baking sheet. Make criss-cross slashes across loaves. Cover and let rise until double. Bake at 400° 30-35 minutes or until done. 2 loaves.

*SOURDOUGH STARTER

1 pkg dry yeast
2 1/2 C warm water

2 C flour
1 T sugar or honey

Dissolve yeast in 1/2 cup water; add rest of ingredients and beat until smooth. Cover with cheesecloth and let stand at room temperature 5-10 days to ferment, stirring 2-3 times a day. (The warmer the room, the faster the process.) Store in refrigerator in a jar covered with cheesecloth, not a tight cover. To use, bring desired amount to room temperature. To replenish starter, stir 3/4 C flour, 3/4 water, and 1 teaspoon sugar into remaining amount and let stand at room temperature for 1 day; store as before. Stir 1 teaspoon sugar into starter every 10 days.

92 PITA BREAD

Low-calorie pockets for your sandwiches

5-51/2 C flour
2 pkg dry yeast
2 C milk

3 T sugar
3 T shortening
2 t salt

In large mixer bowl combine 2 cups flour and yeast. Heat milk, sugar, salt and shortening until warm and shortening is melted. Pour liquids over flour and beat at a low speed for 1 1/2 minutes. Stir in enough of remaining flour to make a stiff dough. Knead on a floured surface until smooth. Place in a greased bowl and raise until doubled. Punch down and let rest 10 minutes. Form dough into balls of desired size and roll each ball flat on an ungreased baking sheet. Bake at 400° until puffed, about 7-9 minutes. Cool on a cloth-covered surface.

93 PRETZELS

In times past, a lenten treat;
let kids make their own shapes

1/2 C warm water
1 pkg dry yeast
1/4 C sugar
1 t salt
1 C milk

1 egg, separated
1/4 C oil (or margarine)
5 C flour
1 T water
coarse salt

Dissolve yeast and sugar in warm water. Mix salt, milk, egg yolk and oil; stir into yeast mixture. Stir in flour to make a stiff dough. Turn dough onto a floured board and knead until smooth and elastic. Place in a greased bowl, and let rise until doubled. Punch dough down and divide into equal pieces. Roll each piece into a rope about 8 inches long. Form into a pretzel shape and place on greased baking sheets. Mix egg white with water and brush pretzels with mixture. Sprinkle lightly with salt. Bake at 475° for 10-12 minutes or until puffed and brown. 12-18 large pretzels.

94 PIZZA

Make your own masterpiece!

Crust: *
2 C flour
1 pkg dry yeast
2/3 C warm water
1 T olive oil or salad oil

Combine ingredients, mix until smooth. Knead for 10 minutes on a floured surface. Cover and let rise for 2 hours. Pat and stretch crust to fit medium pizza pan greased with butter or margarine to make crust crisp. Spread crust with about 1/2 cup pizza sauce of your choice. Top with 8 ounces Mozzarella cheese. Add any combination of toppings: fresh or canned mushrooms, pepperoni, sausage, ham, bacon, green pepper, onion, green or black olives and pineapple. Sprinkle top generously with Parmesan cheese, and a dusting of oregano. Bake on bottom shelf in hot oven 425-450° 7-10 minutes until crust is browned and cheeses melted. Do not overbake. Enjoy!

*1/2 C Parmesan cheese and 1/2 t black pepper can be added to flour mixture for a cheesy crust.

95 ENGLISH MUFFINS

Toast these little beauties and serve with jam

1 C milk, scalded
3 T shortening
2 t salt
2 T sugar

1 C cold water
1 pkg dry yeast
5-6 C flour
corn meal

Combine hot milk, shortening, sugar and salt; stir in cold water and yeast, beating until smooth.* Stir in flour and mix to a stiff dough, kneading until dough can be formed into a ball. Place in a greased bowl and let rise until double. Roll dough 1/2 inch thick on a cornmeal covered board; cut with a floured cutter. Place on an ungreased baking sheet with cornmeal side down and let rise for 15 minutes. With a flat spatula, carefully transfer muffins to a hot ungreased electric frypan or griddle. Bake for 7-10 minutes on each side. Cool. To serve, spilt, toast and butter.
11/2 dozen muffins.

*To make raisin cinnamon muffins, stir in 1/2 C raisins, and 2 t cinnamon before adding remaining flour. Any dried fruit such as currants, cherries or cranberries are also good with or without spice.

96 ENGLISH MUFFIN BREAD

A good after school project for the kids; start to finish in the microwave

2 pkg dry yeast
4 1/2 C flour
1 T sugar
2 t salt

1/4 t baking soda
2 C milk
1/2 C water
1/2 C corn meal

Combine 3 cups flour, yeast, sugar, salt and soda. Heat liquids until very warm; add to dry ingredients and beat well. Add rest of flour and cornmeal. Spoon into two greased glass or microwaveable pans. Cover and let raise 45 minutes. Microwave one loaf at a time for 6 1/2 minutes on high. Let rest for 5 minutes before removing from pans. This bread is very good toasted.

√ Save bread wrappers for your homemade breads; wash, rinse and dry on a broom handle.

97 BAGELS

The homemade flavor is a delight

Basic recipe:
4 1/2 C white flour, or use half white, half wheat or rye flour
1 pkg dry yeast
1 1/2 C warm skim milk, water or other liquid
1 T oil
3 T sugar or honey
2 t salt

Mix 2 C flour and yeast in mixer bowl. Combine water, sugar, salt, and oil and pour into flour; beat with mixer for 2-3 minutes. Stir in enough flour by hand to make a stiff dough.* Turn onto a floured board and and knead until smooth. Cover dough with a towel and let rest for 15 minutes. Cut dough into 12 portions and shape each into a smooth ball; punch a hole in the middle with finger and enlarge hole by stretching the dough. Place formed bagels on a well greased cookie sheet, cover with a towel and let raise 15-20 minutes. Place raised bagels under broiler and brown, turning to brown bottoms. Watch carefully. Bring a Dutch oven, or large

large kettle of water to a boil and add 1 tablespoon sugar. Reduce heat to simmer and put broiled bagels in water; cook about 7 minutes, turning once. Drain on a rack, then place again on greased baking sheet. Bake at 375° for 25-30 minutes. 12 bagels.

*Cinnamon-raisin bagels: Mix 2 teaspoons cinnamon, and 1/3 cup raisins or currants in with flour at this point.
*Onion bagels: Cook 1/3 C chopped onion slowly in 1 tablespoon margarine until tender. Add mixture to batter and stir in well just before adding remaining flour.
*Poppy seed bagels: Add 1 tablespoon poppy seed with flour.

√ Slice bagels and English muffins before freezing; thaw slightly in microwave before toasting. If serving bagels or muffins to a large crowd, toast in oven under broiler.

√ Make individual pizzas with English muffin halves. Spread with pizza sauce, add toppings and broil.

98 HAMBURG BUNS

Makes any sandwich heavenly!

8 C flour
2 pkg dry yeast
2 C warm water
1/2 C oil

1/2 C sugar
1 T salt
3 eggs

Combine half of flour and yeast in large mixer bowl. Combine warm water, oil, sugar and salt. Add to dry mixture, then add eggs. Beat with a mixer for 3 minutes or until smooth. Stir in enough of remaining flour to make a soft dough. Turn onto a floured surface and knead until smooth. Put dough into a greased bowl, cover and let rise until double. Punch down and divide dough into thirds. Let rest for a few minutes. Divide each portion into 8 balls and turn ball in hand, folding edges under to make an even circle. Flatten in hand and place on greased baking sheets, pressing to a 3 1/2 inch circle. Let rise 30 minutes, or until about double. Bake at 375° for 12-15 minutes. Brush tops with melted butter, if desired. These freeze well. Be sure to slice before freezing. 2 dozen rolls.

99 ONION BUNS

Sandwich buns with great taste and color

6 C flour
2 pkg dry yeast
2 1/2 C milk
2 T sugar
4 T instant minced onion (divided)
2 T oil

1 T prepared mustard
1 1/2 t salt
1/4 t pepper
1 egg
1/4 C water

In a large mixer bowl, combine 2 1/2 C flour and yeast. Heat together milk, sugar, *2 tablespoons* onion, oil, mustard, salt and pepper. Pour very warm, but not hot, liquid into flour and beat with mixer for about 3 minutes or until smooth. Stir in enough of remaining flour to make a stiff dough. Turn dough onto a floured board and knead until smooth. Place in a greased bowl and turn once to grease top. Cover and let rise until double. Punch dough down and divide in half. Let rest briefly, then form each portion into 9 balls. Flatten on greased baking sheets in about 3 1/2 inch circles. Let rise until double. Combine 2 tablespoons minced onion with 1/4 C water and let stand for 5 minutes. Beat egg with 2 tablespoons water and brush rolls with egg; sprinkle with onions. Bake at 375° for 20-25 minutes or until done. 18 rolls.

100 BRAN BATTER BUNS

Stir up ahead, refrigerate and bake whenever

2 pkg dry yeast
1 C warm water
2/3 C shortening
3/4 C sugar
1 1/2 t salt

1 C boiling water
1 C all bran
2 eggs, well beaten
6 C sifted flour

Dissolve yeast in warm water and set aside. Combine shortening, sugar, salt and boiling water; stir until shortening is melted; add bran and cool. When mixture is lukewarm, add eggs and yeast. Stir in flour and mix well. Place batter in a greased bowl and grease top. Cover and refrigerate for at least 24 hours. Two hours before baking, remove amount of batter desired and form into rolls or sandwich buns with floured or buttered hands, or spoon into greased muffin cups. Let rise and bake at 375° for 10-12 minutes. Butter tops of hot rolls.

√ Brush buns with mixture of 1 egg and 2 tablespoons water and sprinkle with sesame or poppy seed before baking, if desired.

101   CORN MEAL BUNS

You could get famous for these

1/3 C corn meal
1/2 C sugar
2 t salt
1/2 C shortening
2 C milk
1 pkg dry yeast

1/2 C warm water
2 beaten eggs
4 C flour, or more as needed
melted butter
corn meal

Cook corn meal, sugar, salt, shortening and milk in a medium sauce pan until mixture is consistency of cooked cereal. Cool. Dissolve yeast in water; add to cooled cornmeal mixture. Stir in eggs and flour, mixing thoroughly. Turn onto a floured board and knead until smooth. Place in a greased bowl. (Can be refrigerated at this point; dough will keep for several days.) Let rise until doubled. Roll dough 1 inch thick on a floured board. Cut with a biscuit cutter. Place on a greased baking sheet, brush with melted butter and sprinkle with cornmeal. Cover and let rise until doubled. Bake at 375° for 15 minutes. 12-18 buns.

102 BUTTERMILK RAISED DONUTS

Like some grandmas still make

1 pkg dry yeast
1/4 C warm water
3/4 C scalded buttermilk
1/4 C sugar
1 t salt

1/4 C shortening
1/2 C mashed potato
1 egg, beaten
1 t nutmeg
3 1/2-4 C flour

Dissolve yeast in water. Cool milk to lukewarm. Combine milk with 3 cups flour and remaining ingredients. Using as much additional flour as necessary, knead dough for about 5 minutes or until smooth. Place dough in a greased bowl and let rise until doubled. Turn dough onto a lightly floured board and roll out 1/2 inch thick. Cut with a floured donut cutter and place on a floured surface to raise for about 30-35 minutes. Fry in hot oil until brown on both sides. Drain on paper towels. Roll in granulated sugar. 3-4 dozen donuts.

103 BUTTER HORN ROLLS

Two versions of this old favorite

1 pkg dry yeast
1 C warm water
3 eggs, well beaten
1/2 C melted butter

1 t salt
1/3 C sugar
4 C flour

Dissolve yeast in water and add remaining ingredients in order,
stirring well. Cover with plastic wrap and a towel and refrigerate
overnight. Turn cold dough onto a floured board and roll into a
large circle 1/3-1/2 inch thick. Butter dough, cut in about 40
narrow, pie shaped wedges and roll from wide end to the point.
Place on a greased baking sheet, turning pieces into slight
crescent shapes and let rise until light. (Temperature of dough will
determine raising time.) Bake at 400° for 12-15 minutes or until
lightly browned.

For a delicious sweet roll: After buttering circle, sprinkle lightly
with white sugar, and dot with raisins. Roll and bake as directed
above. Frost with powdered sugar icing.

104 NEVER FAIL SWEET ROLLS

2 pkg dry yeast
2 C lukewarm water
1/2 C sugar
1 T salt

6 1/2 C flour
1/2 C margarine
1 egg

Soften yeast in water; add sugar and salt, melted margarine and eggs. Add 3 C flour and beat well. Add remaining flour and knead until elastic. Place dough in a greased bowl and turn to grease top. Let rise until double. Make cinnamon, pecan rolls or any kind of sweet rolls you desire. Bake at 350° for 15-20 minutes.

105 CINNAMON ROLLS

Probably the best loved sweet rolls of all

*With brown sugar: Roll sweet roll dough into a rectangle. Spread dough with melted butter. Sprinkle generously with brown sugar and cinnamon. Roll as for jelly roll, cut into 11/2 inch pieces and place cut side down in greased 9x13 inch pans. Let rise and bake for 15-20 minutes or until lightly browned. Invert immediately on waxed paper. Frost while warm with powdered sugar icing and sprinkle with nuts, if desired.

With white sugar: Combine 1 1/4 cup sugar, 1/2 cup butter, 3 teaspoons cinnamon in a sauce pan and heat until blended. Spread rolled rectangle with mixture. Add nut meats, raisins or maraschino cherries, if desired. Roll, cut, and bake as above.

106 PECAN ROLLS

Combine 1/3 C margarine, 1/3 C light or dark corn syrup* and 1 cup pecans in a 9x13 inch pan. Place in oven until melted and stir until distributed evenly. (These may also be made in muffin cups for individual rolls.) Make rolls from either recipe above, using less of the toppings. Omit cinnamon, if desired. Cut and place rolls over pecans. Let rise and bake as above. Invert immediately and let syrup and nuts run into rolls.

*Try maple flavored pancake syrup for flavor variety.

107 CAKE MIX CINNAMON ROLLS

An unusual short cut; great to have in the freezer.

1 pkg yellow cake mix, without pudding
2 pkg dry yeast
5 C flour
2 1/2 C hot water

3-5 T soft butter
1 C sugar
2 t cinnamon

Topping:
1/2 C margarine
4 T brown sugar

4 T corn syrup
1 C chopped nuts

Combine cake mix, yeast and flour. Stir in water, mixing well. Cover and let rise until double in bulk. Cut dough in half and roll each half into a rectangle 1/4-1/2 inch thick. Spread with half of softened butter and half of combined cinnamon and sugar. Roll as for a jelly roll and cut into 12, 2 inch slices. Place rolls in two greased 9x13 inch pans. Let rise until double. Just before baking, heat topping ingredients until margarine is melted. Spoon over rolls. Bake at 375° for 25 minutes. 24 rolls. These freeze well.

108 QUICKY STICKY BUNS

*One popular sixth grade teacher makes these
for her students every year!*

5 C flour
3 T sugar
2 t salt
1 t soda
3 t baking powder

1/2 C margarine
2 T warm water
1 pkg dry yeast
2 C warmed buttermilk
Topping:
margarine
brown or white sugar
cinnamon

Combine dry ingredients and cut in shortening as for pie crust.
Dissolve yeast in water and add buttermilk. Stir milk into flour
mixture until blended. Turn out on floured board and knead
enough to hold dough together. (Can be refrigerated at this point
to bake later.) Roll dough into a rectangle and spread with melted
margarine. Sprinkle liberally with either brown or white sugar and
cinnamon. Roll as for jelly roll, slice and place in greased baking
pans. Bake **without raising** at 400° for 10-15 minutes. Invert on
waxed paper. Frost if desired. 2 1/2 dozen rolls.

109 SWEDISH TEA RING

3 1/2-4 C flour
1 pkg dry yeast
1 C milk
1/2 C sugar (divided)
1 t salt

1 egg
2 T oil
2 T melted butter
1 t cinnamon
3/4 C chopped pecans

Combine flour and yeast in mixer bowl. Heat milk, 1/4 cup sugar, oil and salt until warm, but not hot. Pour into flour mixture, add egg and beat with mixer for 3 minutes. Stir in enough of remaining flour to make a soft dough. Turn onto a floured surface and knead until smooth. Place in a greased bowl and turn to grease top. Let rise until doubled. Punch down and divide dough in half. Roll each half into an 8x12 inch rectangle. Spread with melted butter. Mix remaining sugar, cinnamon and nuts and sprinkle over dough. Roll each rectangle from the 12 inch side jelly roll style. Shape into rings, sealing ends and place on greased baking sheets. Snip ring at one inch intervals almost to center and twist sections until a fan shape ring is shaped. Let rise until almost double. Bake at 375° for about 25 minutes or until golden. Cool and frost with powdered sugar icing and decorate with maraschino cherries and pecans. 2 tea rings.

110 SOUR CREAM TWISTS

Easy, rich and delicious

4 C flour
1 t salt
1 C margarine
1 pkg dry yeast
1/4 C warm water

1 egg + 2 yolks
1 C sour cream
1 t vanilla
3/4 C sugar
cinnamon-sugar mixture

Mix salt with flour in a bowl and cut in margarine with a pastry cutter. Dissolve yeast in warm water. Beat egg with yolks and combine with yeast, sour cream and vanilla. Add egg mixture to flour and mix well with a fork. Cover with foil and let rise for 2 hours in refrigerator. Turn dough onto floured board and roll into a rectangle. Sprinkle with one fourth of sugar; fold dough roll again and sprinkle with sugar again; repeat twice more. Roll dough again 1/2 inch thick. Cut into 2x5 inch strips, twist strips and place on a greased baking sheet. Bake at 375° for 15-20 minutes. Sprinkle with cinnamon sugar.

111 CRISPY COFFEE CAKES

An easy Danish-type pastry; quick, no raising

4 C flour
1 t salt
1 t grated lemon rind
1/4 C sugar
1 C margarine

1 C milk, scalded
1/4 C warm water
1 pkg dry yeast
2 beaten eggs
1 C sugar
1 T cinnamon

Combine flour, salt, lemon rind and 1/4 cup sugar; cut in margarine with a pastry blender. Dissolve yeast in warm water and add mixture to cooled milk; stir in eggs. Pour liquid ingredients over flour mixture and mix with a fork until blended. Cover tightly and chill or several hours or overnight. Divide dough in half and roll each half on a floured board as for pie crust. Mix 1 cup sugar and cinnamon and spread half over each half of dough. Roll up as for cinnamon rolls (dough will be sticky, so use flour and a knife to help with the rolling). Cut rolls 1 inch thick and place cut side down on greased cookie sheets. Flatten each piece with floured hand. Bake, without raising, at 400° for 12 minutes or until delicately brown. Remove immediately from pans. Frost with powdered sugar icing.

112 CASSEROLE SWEET BREAD

A round frosted loaf with raisins

1/2 C boiling water
3 T shortening
1 t salt
1/4 C sugar
1/2 C evaporated milk

1 pkg dry yeast
2 eggs, beaten
1/2 C chopped walnuts
1/2 C seedless raisins
3 1/4 C flour

Pour boiling water over shortening and stir until dissolved; stir in salt, sugar and milk. Dissolve yeast in 1/4 C water and stir into mixture. Add eggs, nuts, raisins and half of the flour; beat until smooth. Stir in remaining flour. Cover and let rise until double, about 1 1/2 hours. Punch down and place in a greased 2 quart casserole; cover and let rise again until nearly double. Bake at 375° for one hour or until done. Cool on rack and frost if desired.

Frosting: Combine 2/3 C powdered sugar, 1 T evaporated milk, and 1/2 t vanilla. Spread on cooled bread and sprinkle with chopped nuts.

113 HOT CROSS BUNS

A favorite Easter Sweet

1 pkg dry yeast
4 T warm water
1 1/2 C scalded milk
6 T butter or margarine
1/2 C sugar (white or brown)

1/2 C currants
1 t salt
2 t cinnamon
1 egg
2 1/4 C flour

Dissolve yeast in water and set aside. Combine milk, butter, sugar, salt and cinnamon; cool to lukewarm and add yeast mixture. Add eggs, currants and flour. Mix and then knead well. Place in a greased bowl, cover and let rise until double. Form dough into about 2 dozen balls and place on a greased baking sheet about 1 1/2 inches apart. Cut a deep cross in top of each ball with floured scissors. Cover and let rise again until double. Bake at 375° for 20 minutes. Brush warm rolls with syrup or pipe white icing in cross.

*Syrup: Boil 1/4 C sugar with 2 T milk for one minute.

114 ORANGE ROLLS

Unforgettable flavor

Dough:
2 pkgs dry yeast
1 T sugar
1/2 C sugar
1/4 C shortening
2 t salt
1 C boiling water
3/4 C cold water
2 eggs
7 1/2 C flour

Syrup:
1/2 C butter
2 C sugar
1 C orange juice and pulp
2-3 T grated orange rind

melted butter

Combine syrup ingredients and boil for 6 minutes, stirring constantly. Divide mixture into muffin cups, using 1 tablespoon per cup. Dissolve yeast in 1/2 C lukewarm water and add 1 tablespoon sugar. Combine 1/2 cup sugar, shortening, salt and boiling water. Cool with 3/4 cup cold water. Beat in eggs and yeast mixture. Stir in flour and knead until dough is smooth and elastic. Roll dough, 1/3 at a time into a 10X12 inch rectangle. Brush with melted butter. Roll, starting at 12 inch edge. Cut into 1 inch slices and place a slice in each muffin cup. Let rise until double. Bake at 375° for 15-20 minutes. Let stand for a minute and then invert and let syrup run through rolls. 24-30 rolls.

The Grand Cook Book Series

The Big Fat Red Juicy Apple Cook Book
Tasty Taters
Cherry Time!
Say Cheese
Fish Food
The Very Berry Cook Book
Merry Cookie
BBQ Cooking
Daily Bread
Just Peachy
Salad Chef